COUNTRY 🌐 PROFILES

CUBA

BY AMY RECHNER

BLASTOFF! DISCOVERY

Blastoff! Discovery launches a new mission: reading to learn. Filled with facts and features, each book offers you an exciting new world to explore!

This edition first published in 2019 by Bellwether Media, Inc.

No part of this publication may be reproduced in whole or in part without written permission of the publisher.
For information regarding permission, write to Bellwether Media, Inc., Attention: Permissions Department,
6012 Blue Circle Drive, Minnetonka, MN 55343.

Library of Congress Cataloging-in-Publication Data

Names: Rechner, Amy, author.
Title: Cuba / by Amy Rechner.
Description: Minneapolis, MN : Bellwether Media, Inc., 2019. | Series: Blastoff! Discovery: Country Profiles | Includes bibliographical references and index.
Identifiers: LCCN 2018000616 (print) | LCCN 2018001146 (ebook) | ISBN 9781626178403 (hardcover : alk. paper) | ISBN 9781681035819 (ebook)
Subjects: LCSH: Cuba–Juvenile literature.
Classification: LCC F1758.5 (ebook) | LCC F1758.5 .R43 2019 (print) | DDC 972.91–dc23
LC record available at https://lccn.loc.gov/2018000616

Editor: Rebecca Sabelko   Designer: Brittany McIntosh

Printed in the United States of America, North Mankato, MN.

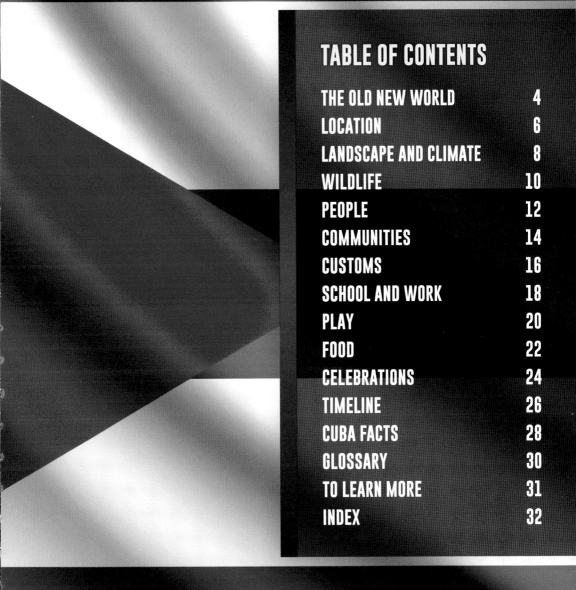

TABLE OF CONTENTS

OLD HAVANA

A family of **tourists** walks the narrow streets of Old Havana. Some of the brightly colored buildings have stood since the 1500s. Tempting smells and lively music pour out of open doors. Old cars and horse-drawn carts rumble by on cobblestone streets.

OTHER TOP SITES

AMBROSIO CAVE

MORRO CASTLE

SAN PEDRO DE LA ROCA CASTLE

VALLEY DE LOS INGENIOS

They visit a colonial **fort** at the **Plaza** de Armas, followed by the *Museo de la Ciudad*, or City Museum. After exploring the *Catedral de La Habana*, or Havana Cathedral, everyone is ready for ice cream. They sit on the Malecón, the seawall bordering Havana's harbor. Musicians play guitars as groups chatter nearby. People dance in the afternoon sun. This is Cuba!

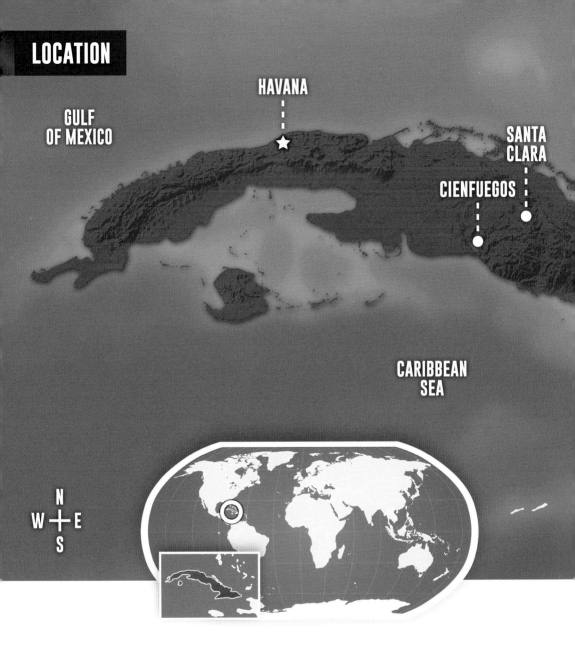

HAVANA

GULF
OF MEXICO

SANTA
CLARA

CIENFUEGOS

CARIBBEAN
SEA

N
W + E
S

Cuba is an island nation that covers 42,803 square miles (110,860 square kilometers) of land. Havana, the capital, sits along the northwestern coast. The Atlantic Ocean surrounds Cuba to the north and the east. The southern coast is washed by the waters of the Caribbean Sea. The Gulf of Mexico lies to the west.

BAHAMAS

NEAR NEIGHBORS

Cuba is only 90 miles (145 kilometers) away from Florida to the north. Mexico is 135 miles (217 kilometers) to the west.

ATLANTIC OCEAN

CUBA

SANTIAGO DE CUBA

Cuba is the largest island in the **West Indies**. Its neighboring islands are Jamaica, the Cayman Islands, the Bahamas, and Hispaniola, which includes Haiti and the Dominican Republic.

The waters surrounding Cuba are filled with hundreds of smaller islands. The seas splash upon white sand beaches. Bays and inlets create natural harbors. **Coral reefs** and saltwater

= SIERRA MAESTRA MOUNTAINS

mangrove swamps line the coast. Rocky coastlines and forested mountain ranges protect rolling and flat **plains**. The Sierra Maestra Mountains march along much of the southeastern coast.

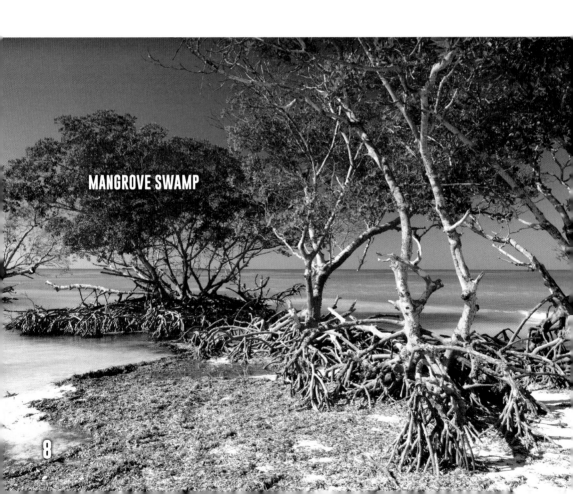

MANGROVE SWAMP

SIERRA MAESTRA
MOUNTAINS

HOME IN THE TROPICS

Cuba's location on the globe is below an imaginary line called the Tropic of Cancer. The area between the Tropic of Cancer and the equator is part of an area called the tropics.

HAVANA

Average seasonal highs and lows

JANUARY
HIGH: 78 °F (26 °C)
LOW: 66 °F (19 °C)

APRIL
HIGH: 83 °F (29 °C)
LOW: 70 °F (21 °C)

JULY
HIGH: 88 °F (31 °C)
LOW: 75 °F (24 °C)

OCTOBER
HIGH: 85 °F (29 °C)
LOW: 73 °F (23 °C)

°F = degrees Fahrenheit
°C = degrees Celsius

Cuba's **tropical** climate is mild all year. The weather is dry and cool from November to April. May through October is hot and rainy. Hurricanes are a yearly threat. Their strong winds and heavy rain are most dangerous from June to November.

WILDLIFE

Cuba is home to wildlife that cannot be found anywhere else. Rare bee hummingbirds live in Cuba's dense forests. Eastern red bats roost in the trees. Rat-like animals called solenodons are considered one of the most unusual mammals in the world!

Manatees float through shallow freshwaters and coastal areas. Cuban crocodiles lurk in the Zapata Swamp or wander its shores. Sharks and barracudas swim in the warm seas. Flamingos and egrets wade in the shallows looking for food.

EASTERN RED BAT

AMERICAN MANATEE

CUBAN TROGON

FLYING COLORS

Cuba's national bird is the *tocororo*, or Cuban trogon. Its red, white, and blue feathers match the colors of the nation's flag.

BEE HUMMINGBIRD

CUBAN
CROCODILE

CUBAN
CROCODILE

Life Span: 50-75 years
Red List Status: critically endangered

Cuban crocodile range = ■

LEAST CONCERN	NEAR THREATENED	VULNERABLE	ENDANGERED	CRITICALLY ENDANGERED	EXTINCT IN THE WILD	EXTINCT

COMBINING RELIGIONS

Santería combines praying to Catholic saints and African spirits. Rituals include rhythmic music and chanting prayer.

The small island of Cuba is home to more than 11 million people. The majority of the population come from the Spanish colonists. Ten percent of the people have **ancestors** who were African **slaves**. They were brought to Cuba over many centuries until the country's slave trade ended in 1867. More than one in four Cubans come from both Europeans and Africans.

The official language spoken in Cuba is Spanish. But the language has some **Creole** influences. Christianity is widely practiced in Cuba. Most people are Catholic but others are Protestant. Santería, an old, West African-based religion founded in Cuba, is also practiced.

FAMOUS FACE

Name: Kcho (Alexis Leiva Machado)
Birthday: February 12, 1970
Hometown: Nueva Gerona, Cuba
Famous for: An artist who introduced the first free Wi-Fi service in Havana

SPEAK SPANISH

ENGLISH	SPANISH	HOW TO SAY IT
hello	hola	OH-lah
goodbye	adiós	ah-dee-OHS
please	por favor	pohr fah-VOR
thank you	gracias	grah-SEE-ahs
yes	sí	SEE
no	no	noh

HAVANA

The capital city of Havana is very crowded. Many buildings are old, bright, and unique. Their shapes and colors show the Spanish history of the city. Traditional **rural** houses in the country have **thatched roofs** and dirt floors. Since family is an important part of Cuban life, extended families usually live in homes nearby.

DRIVE THRU HISTORY

Classic American cars from the 1950s cruise the streets of Havana. Their owners take good care of them. They often offer rides in the cars as a special taxi service.

Cuba has a long highway across the island, but not many people own cars. Most cars in Cuba are very old. People take buses or ride bicycles. Some ride in horse-drawn carts. Trains connecting the cities are old and often very slow.

Cuban **culture** is an exciting blend of the African and Spanish cultures. The people of Cuba are warm and welcoming. Singing and dancing are part of daily life for children and adults. Music is playing wherever people are together.

Social gatherings are common. Cubans like being with other people. Since homes are small, friends usually meet outdoors for conversation. Men are greeted with a handshake and women give a kiss on the cheek. Time with friends is relaxed. Many meet at sports events or over a meal.

CHA-CHA-CHA!

Cuban dance music hit the United States in the 1950s. Mambo records by Cuban bandleaders made the music popular. The dances are still on display in ballroom dance performances.

Cuba has one of the highest **literacy** rates in the world! Children attend primary school through sixth grade. After completing middle school around age 14, students can choose to go to secondary school or trade school. Many students study subjects involving technology, agriculture, and education.

Almost three-quarters of Cubans work in **service jobs**. People find work in the government, education, and healthcare. Many work in tourism, too. Farmers grow crops such as sugarcane and tobacco. Factory workers turn the sugarcane into other products like molasses and syrup. Machinery and chemical products are often produced, too.

SUGARCANE FARMERS

SERVING THEIR COUNTRY

After high school, men must complete two years of military service before they turn 28 years old. Women get to decide if they want to serve in the military.

BRINGING HOME THE GOLD!

There are no professional sports teams in Cuba, but its athletes still excel. Cuba's Olympic baseball team brought home three gold and two silver medals in five straight Summer Olympics.

Baseball is an important part of life in Cuba. Cubans follow the baseball season closely and excitedly discuss the games with friends and strangers. Young children play stickball in the streets. Kids and adults all enjoy playing catch or a pickup game wherever there is a field to play on.

Soccer is gaining fans, too. Young boys learn to box, while girls take up volleyball. Many learn to dance and play guitar at home. Dominoes is played by many. It is often called Cuba's other national pastime. Working adults get a full month off each year. Their vacations are spent on beaches or relaxing at home.

DOMINOES

STICKBALL

What You Need:
- two teams of 3-4 players
- a stick, such as a broom handle
- a small, bouncy ball, such as a tennis ball
- an open playground

How to Play:
1. Street stickball uses manhole covers as home plate and second base. Find a landmark on your playground for home plate, and set up the rest of the "field" from there. You can use backpacks or lunch boxes for bases.

2. The rules of the game are the same as baseball, except each batter only gets two strikes before being called "out," and foul balls are counted as "out" right away.

3. Choose which team bats first. Pitch underhanded so the ball bounces once before the batter tries to hit it.

4. You can play as many innings as you would like!

Cuban food blends the strong flavors of Latin and African **cuisines**. The Cuban diet depends on *moros y cristianos*, or beans and rice, seasoned with onions, garlic, and peppers. Pork, root vegetables, and eggs add variety to the dinner table.

Breakfast includes fruit, eggs, and buttered tostadas with *café con leche*, or coffee with milk. Lunch is often a quick *empanada*, or sandwich, made with chicken, beef, or ham. The main meal is dinner. *Ajiaco*, a meat and vegetable stew, is often served with beans and rice. A favorite dessert is *natilla*, or vanilla pudding.

EMPANADA

AJIACO

ARROZ CON LECHE RECIPE

Ingredients:
2 1/4 cups water
1 cup uncooked rice
1/4 teaspoon ground cinnamon
1/2 cup sugar
1 tablespoon flour
1/2 teaspoon salt
1 cup milk
1/4 cup raisins
sprinkle of ground cinnamon for topping

Steps:
1. With the help of an adult, boil the water in a large saucepan. Pour in the rice, stir, and reduce the heat to a simmer. Cover the saucepan until the rice is fully cooked.

2. Once rice is fully cooked, add the ground cinnamon, and fluff the rice with a fork.

3. In a medium-size bowl, mix the sugar, flour, and salt.

4. Add the milk slowly to the sugar mixture. Stir until the sugar is mixed into the milk.

5. Slowly pour the milk mixture into the rice. Keep stirring the rice while you pour in the milk. Add cinnamon and raisins and enjoy!

CELEBRATIONS

CARNIVAL

The most important holidays in Cuba celebrate the country's modern history. January 1 is Liberation Day. Cubans celebrate the beginning of the **Communist** government. People fill the streets to enjoy live music and dancing.

The biggest holiday is Revolution Day on July 26. Thousands of people gather in Havana and Santiago de Cuba for three-day street festivals that include parades, costumes, dancing, and feasts. Around that same time is Carnival, an Afro-Cuban festival. Carnival began as a harvest celebration on sugarcane **plantations**. Today, music and dancing are the main activities. Cubans spend time with family and friends, remember their history, and celebrate their culture!

REVOLUTION DAY

800–200 BCE
Waves of Taíno people inhabit the Caribbean Islands, including Puerto Rico, Jamaica, and Cuba

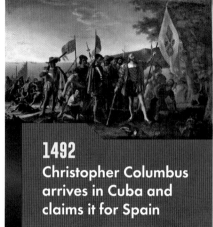

1492
Christopher Columbus arrives in Cuba and claims it for Spain

1776
During the American Revolution, American ships buy supplies in Cuban ports

1898
Cuba gains its independence under American protection under the terms of the Treaty of Paris

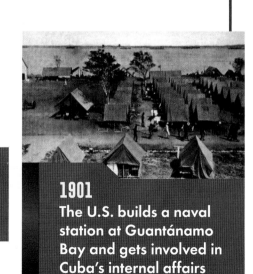

1901
The U.S. builds a naval station at Guantánamo Bay and gets involved in Cuba's internal affairs

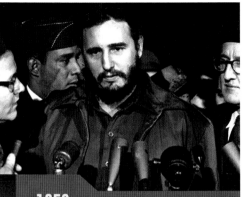

1961
The U.S. tries and fails to overthrow Castro in an operation known as the Bay of Pigs

1959
Fidel Castro leads a guerrilla army into Havana, becomes the leader of the government, and guides Cuba into Communism

1962
In what is now known as the Cuban Missile Crisis, the Soviet Union ships nuclear missiles to Cuba as a threat to the U.S.

2008
Fidel Castro steps down as president due to ill health, and his brother, Raúl Castro, takes over

2016
President Barack Obama visits Cuba after working to improve U.S.-Cuban relations and becomes the first American president to visit since 1928

CUBA FACTS

Official Name: Republic of Cuba

Flag of Cuba: The Cuban flag consists of five stripes, blue alternating with white. To the left is a red triangle with a white, five-pointed star in the center. The triangle symbolizes liberty, equality, and brotherhood. The red stands for bloodshed in the fight for independence. The white star lights the way to freedom.

Area: 42,803 square miles
(110,860 square kilometers)

Capital City: Havana

Important Cities: Santiago de Cuba, Santa Clara, Cienfuegos

Population:
11,147,407 (July 2017)

WHERE PEOPLE LIVE

COUNTRYSIDE
22.7%

CITY
77.3%

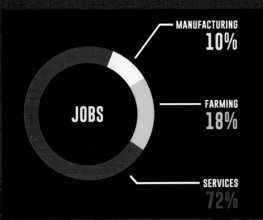

MANUFACTURING
10%

JOBS

FARMING
18%

SERVICES
72%

Main Exports:

petroleum   nickel   tobacco

sugar   medical products

National Holiday:
Liberation Day (January 1)

Main Language:
Spanish

Form of Government:
Communist state

Title for Country Leaders:
president of the council of state and
president of the council of ministers

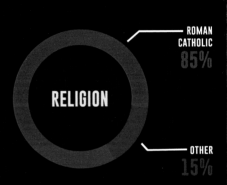

RELIGION

ROMAN CATHOLIC
85%

OTHER
15%

Unit of Money:
Cuban peso

GLOSSARY

ancestors—relatives who lived long ago

Communist—related to Communism; Communism is a social system in which property and goods are controlled by the government.

coral reefs—structures made of coral that usually grow in shallow seawater

Creole—relating to a person of European background who was born in the West Indies

cuisines—styles of cooking

culture—the beliefs, arts, and ways of life in a place or society

fort—a protected place for an army

literacy—the ability to read and write

mangrove—a tree or shrub that grows in swamps

plains—large areas of flat land

plantations—large farms that grow coffee beans, cotton, rubber, or other crops; plantations are mainly found in warm climates.

plaza—a public square in a city or town

rural—related to the countryside

service jobs—jobs that perform tasks for people or businesses

slaves—people who work for no pay and are considered property

thatched roofs—roofs with coverings made of grass or straw

tourists—people who travel to visit another place

tropical—part of the tropics; the tropics is a hot, rainy region near the equator.

West Indies—the islands between southeastern North America and northern South America in the Caribbean Sea

TO LEARN MORE

AT THE LIBRARY

Fabiny, Sarah. *Who Was Fidel Castro?* New York, N.Y.: Penguin Workshop, 2017.

Kent, Deborah. *Cuba*. New York, N.Y.: Children's Press, 2016.

Sheehan, Sean. *Cuba*. New York, N.Y.: Cavendish Square, 2016.

ON THE WEB

Learning more about Cuba is as easy as 1, 2, 3.

1. Go to www.factsurfer.com.

2. Enter "Cuba" into the search box.

3. Click the "Surf" button and you will see a list of related web sites.

With factsurfer.com, finding more information is just a click away.

INDEX

The images in this book are reproduced through the courtesy of: Lena Wurm, front cover; Hang Dinh, pp. 4-5; Minikhan, p. 5 (top); Kamira, pp. 5 (middle top), 9 (bottom), 15, 24; Inspired By Maps, p. 5 (middle bottom); Milosz Maslanka, p. 5 (bottom); Capture Light, p. 8; Matyas Rehak, p. 9 (top); Chris Harshaw/ Wikipedia, p. 10 (top); Vladimir Wrangel, p. 10 (middle top); Sergey Uryadnikov, p. 10 (middle bottom); Melinda Fawver, pp. 10 (bottom), 12; Gudkov Andrey, p. 11; Alberto Reyes/ Newscom, p. 13 (top); Photoillustrator, p. 13 (bottom); BonnieBC, p. 14; akturer, p. 16; Kobby Dagan, p. 17; dov makabaw Cuba/ Alamy, p. 18; possohh, p. 19 (top); PhotosByByron, p. 19 (bottom); Donald Miralle/ Getty, p. 20 (top); Nikada, p. 20 (bottom); Diego Cervo, p. 21 (top); Africa Studio, p. 21 (bottom left); Kapustin Igor, p. 21 (bottom right); Hemis/ Alamy, p. 22; yasuhiro amano, p. 23 (top); Larisa Blinova, p. 23 (middle); Belish, p. 23 (bottom); Andrey Zheludev, p. 25; Panther/ Wikipedia, p. 26 (top left); Architect of the Capitol/ Wikipedia, p. 26 (top right); Unknown/ Wikipedia, p. 26 (bottom); U.S. News & World Report/ Wikipedia, p. 27 (top); Chuck Kennedy/ Wikipedia, p. 27 (bottom); Claudio Divizia, p. 29 (left); Yaroslaff, p. 29 (right).